uide

ZOOM MEETINGS

A Guide for the Non-Techie

By
Jane Tabachnick

Published by Plain Jane's Guide, an imprint of Simply Good Press
Montclair, NJ
info@simplygoodpress.com

ISBN: 978-1-7326521-8-7 (eBook)
ISBN: 978-1-7326521-7-0 (Paperback)
ISBN: 978-1-7326521-9-4 (Epub)

Library of Congress Control Number: 2020906255

Photo credits: Keri Budinger

I'm glad that you are here. This book is designed to help you understand and get comfortable with online conferencing and the Zoom platform, even if you don't like or aren't comfortable with technology.

The book is created as a training guide and a desktop companion. We talk about the Zoom software and have also included a lot of screenshots so that you can see what we are describing in the text. When it comes to learning a new technology, it's especially true that a picture is worth a thousand words.

There are a few important things to note before you start reading the book:

We have shared with you the most up to date information available at the time of the publication of this guide.

By the time you are reading this, the software may have gone through updates and changes. Most software gets updated and changed regularly. This can include changes in features, the layout of the user interface and dashboard, as well as pricing plans.

In this guide, we don't cover the different service levels/pricing plans available with Zoom. That is because they may also change at any time. It is possible that a feature we cover is only available in the paid version or a higher level of service than you are using. It will ultimately be up to you to check what features come with your plan.

As you are reading this book, and following along on your own device you may wonder: **Why does my screen look different than what you show in your guide?**

There are several possible reasons including:

- Zoom has had an update and changed the layout or features

- You are subscribed to a different service level
- You are viewing Zoom on a different device than what we show [our screenshots are all taken from the desktop/laptop view]
- You have chosen a different 'view' once in a Zoom meeting room

Happy Zooming
Jane Tabachnick

Table of Contents

1

Introduction

Zoom is a useful platform that's used by people around the world to host video conferences, webinars, and online presentations. Using it, employers can easily connect with employees, professors and teachers can provide lectures to students, entrepreneurs can even host paid webinars that teach others about specific topics, and friends and family can connect online. Although Zoom meetings are attended live or virtually "in person," they can be recorded for future reference. Those who couldn't attend in person can also view the replay to learn what they missed.

Why Is Zoom Important?

Zoom connects coworkers and colleagues together online. In a world where people are becoming frequently interconnected no matter where they live and work, it's important to know how to use the platform successfully. Look at it this way – a company may have its headquarters in Seattle with a satellite office in Chicago. How are those workers going to team up on projects and interface with each other? The short answer here is Zoom.

The creators of the Zoom platform developed a useful and easy way to communicate using the cloud. If you work for a company that has remote employees or own a business that requires the use of virtual presentations and webinars, then this is the tool that you should be using.

While it was designed for business use, Zoom can be a great platform for connecting with friends and family online.

Why You Need to Know How to Use Zoom

As the popularity of Zoom rises, the likelihood that you'll need to join a meeting or use the platform to attend a webinar goes up as well. To come across as professional while doing so, you need to know the ins and outs of attending these scheduled events.

Also, you may find yourself on the other side, as the person hosting the meeting or webinar. Once again, you'll want to make sure that everything runs smoothly and is handled professionally. Knowing as much as possible about Zoom is the first step towards ensuring that your first meetings – as well as all the others afterward – go well.

What We'll Cover Here

As the title implies, we'll cover a lot of the main features of Zoom, from attending events to hosting them. Things like how to set up an account, hosting a webinar, recording your meetings, and even how to dress and how to behave professionally on Zoom are covered. You'll learn everything that you need to know to get started, as well as some of the more advanced features.

Part 1

Zoom Basics and Usage

2

The Basics

Zoom is an online, cloud-based platform that helps businesses connect with clients, employees, and potential partners, no matter where they're located in the world. Zoom is quickly becoming one of the most popular options for these meetings because it's easy to use and includes many different features.

What Zoom Does

When someone sets up a Zoom call and other people join in, Zoom creates what's called a Zoom room. This is a type of virtual conference room that contains all the other attendees. Within the Zoom room, screens can be shared with the group, making it easy to follow along with what's being communicated.

There are different types of Zoom users. As a participant, you don't need your own Zoom account. You can attend for free unless it is a paid event. A free account will allow you to host meetings, though there are attendee and time limits on the account.

Paid accounts have a few different plan levels, each with their own set of features. Check with Zoom for the latest plan offers.

Not only does Zoom make it easy for people to connect with each other, but one of its functionalities involves allowing hosts the ability to record their meetings. It's also possible to have the platform create a transcription of the recording for those who prefer to read the content that was shared instead of listening to it.

Finally, Zoom allows meeting hosts to customize their backgrounds on the platform. Rather than showing everything that's behind the host, from their home office to their business office space, they can choose a different background from one of Zoom's many options. This makes it easy to customize the conference call with a company's branding or keep personal, unprofessional, spaces as private and hidden as possible. Attendees can customize their backgrounds if the meeting host has enabled this feature for them.

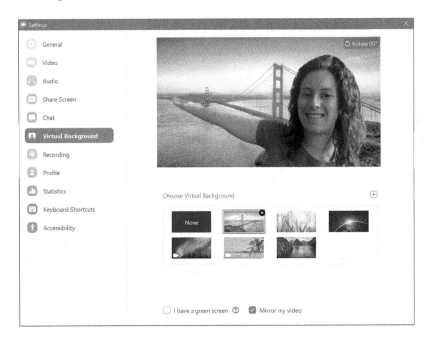

How to Communicate with Others on Zoom

There are several different methods of communicating with others on Zoom. They include:

Using the platform to speak verbally – Both the person (or people) hosting the meeting and the attendees can speak to each other through Zoom. There are ways to mute microphones and control who can talk and who can listen, making it easier for those in attendance to follow along.

Chatting during a meeting – Attendees can chat with one another on a central chat board within the Zoom room. Anyone in attendance can see these messages and respond to them.

Private messaging – There's also a private messaging function within Zoom. The host can send a single message to one person in attendance or to everyone, although only the people who it was sent to can see it. The attendees can also send private messages to one another that the host can't see.

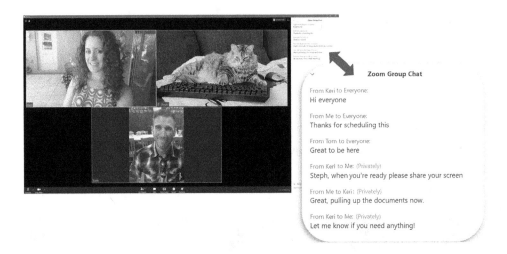

The host has the power to control who can chat and which methods of communication can be used. For example, the central chat board can be turned off or it can set so that only the host can send and receive private messages. It all depends on whether the host thinks that these lines of communication will be disruptive.

3

Participating in a Meeting

One of the best things about Zoom is the fact that anyone can attend a meeting. You don't have to have a Zoom account – just the meeting ID number. This means that a company can, for example, use Zoom to interview a potential candidate for a job without requiring them to be a paid user or giving them an account with the company.

How to Access a Meeting

You need two things to access a Zoom meeting: internet or phone access and a Zoom meeting ID or teleconferencing number. Every Zoom meeting has a special ID number that consists of either nine, ten, or eleven digits.

Zoom can be accessed in the following ways:

By Phone

To join a Zoom meeting by phone, you need to have a teleconferencing number. This number should be provided to you by the person who scheduled the meeting and will be in your invitation.

Step 1: Dial the provided main phone number.

Step 2: When prompted, enter the teleconferencing number.

Keep in mind that joining a meeting in this way only gives you access to the audio portion of the call. If you'd like to see the visual portion from your phone, you'll need to use the Android or iPhone app.

Windows or Apple Web Browser

A popular way to view a scheduled Zoom conference call, using your web browser requires the use of your computer's camera and microphone.

If you go to Zoom in your web browser:

Step 1: Go to the Zoom website.

Step 2: Click on "Join a Meeting"

Step 3: Enter the meeting ID number

Step 4: Enter your name

You may be prompted at some point during this process to download the Zoom browser plugin. This will make it easier for you to join Zoom meetings in the future.

If you have the Zoom browser plugin downloaded to your computer:

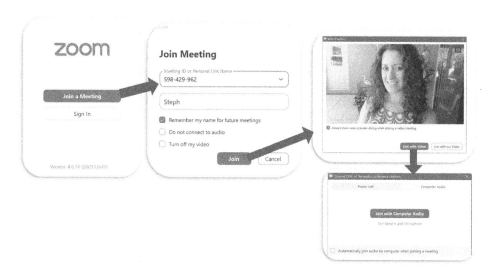

Step 1: Open the app

Step 2: Follow the prompts to either login or join a meeting.

Step 3: Enter the meeting ID number

Step 4: Enter your name (note: if you're logged into your Zoom account, the system will automatically populate your name, so you can skip this step.)

Android

You can also access a Zoom meeting from anywhere, thanks to the Zoom mobile app for Android phones. Download it from the Google Play store, and then follow these prompts to join your conference call:

Step 1: Open the app

Step 2: Follow the prompts to either login or join a meeting.

Step 3: Enter the meeting ID number

Step 4: Enter your name (note: if you're logged into your Zoom account, the system will automatically populate your name, so you can skip this step.)

Step 5: Choose whether you want to access the meeting via audio-only or with audio and video. Once you've made your decision, click on "Join meeting" once again.

iPhone

There's also a Zoom app for iPhones and iPads. Download the app from the iTunes store and then follow the prompts to gain access to your meeting.

Step 1: Open the app

Step 2: Follow the prompts to either login or join a meeting.

Step 3: Enter the meeting ID number

Step 4: Enter your name (note: if you're logged into your Zoom account, the system will automatically populate your name, so you can skip this step.)

Step 5: Choose whether you want to access the meeting via audio-only or with audio and video. Once you've made your decision, click on "Join meeting" once again.

Additional Access Methods

On top of the most common ways to join in a Zoom meeting or webinar, you can use the Linux operating system, which then uses your web browser. The instructions for this process are the same as they are for the Windows or Apple web browser.

Zoom Tools for Attendees

Although hosts have access to the Zoom dashboard, which is set up to handle many functions, attendees do have some options. There are several important tools for these attendees that give you some control over which portions of the meeting you can see and hear while the meeting is in session.

Audio Controls

The "mute" and "unmute" button allows you to control whether the other people on the call can hear you.

Clicking on the up arrow or caret ^ next to the mute/unmute button gives you control over the speaker and microphone. With it, you can change the audio settings, switch from the built-in speaker to a plug-in one, or turn off the computer audio altogether.

Shortcuts: Instead of clicking the buttons on the screen, you can use the following keyboard shortcuts to mute the audio on your end, leaving the other attendees unable to hear you.

Windows: Alt + A

Mac: Shift + Command + A

If you want to speak, but have the microphone muted, you can press the spacebar key on either type of computer. This will "unmute" your microphone as long as the key is held down. Once you release it, your microphone will be muted again.

Video Controls

Using the video controls, you can control the camera on your computer, preventing other attendees from seeing you. Note that this doesn't affect the audio, so you'll still be able to hear the host and other attendees.

Clicking the "start video" and "stop video" button turns your computer's camera either on or off.

Clicking on the up arrow or caret ^ next to the start/stop video button gives you control over the camera that Zoom has access to. With it, you can change the background to a virtual one included by the program (if the host allows you to do so), switch from one camera to another that's also attached to your computer or device, or turn off the video altogether.

Additional Controls

On top of the important audio and video controls, there are several other controls that Zoom meeting attendees may need to use.

Participants

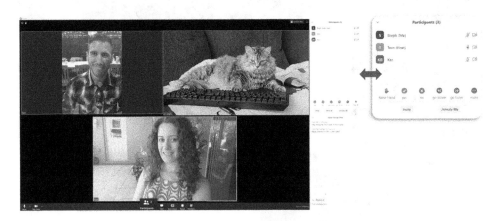

This option allows you to see who is currently attending the meeting. It's useful for employees who aren't hosting that may be tasked with taking attendance at a company meeting. Attendees will also be able to see the participants list. You can also click on the "invite" button allows you to invite other people to join the meeting if the host allows it.

Zoom Room Layouts

As an attendee, you have a variety of layout options available to you. On your desktop, the layout selection is on the top right corner of your Zoom room.

These are screen layout options available: Active Speaker, Gallery, and Mini or Thumbnail view. These layouts are available if screen sharing is not being used.

Speaker   Thumbnail   Gallery

You also can view your Zoom meeting in full screen mode on any of the layouts, with the exception of the Mini view. To go full screen, you click on the icon with four arrows on the top right corner of your Zoom window. To exit full screen, you can press the Exit Full Screen button or press the Esc key on your keyboard.

Here are some examples of different Zoom room views:

Full screen Speaker View

Speaker View

Gallery View with screen sharing

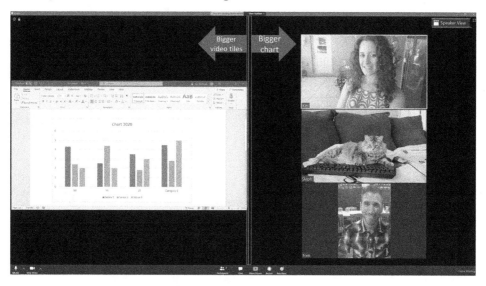

Speaker View with screen sharing

Rename

If you want to change your screen name for any reason, you can do so by hovering over your name on the screen and clicking on the "rename" option that appears.

Feedback Icons

The host of every session has the ability to allow attendees to use what are non-verbal feedback icons. You can change the icon that's next to your name in order to get the host's attention, such as if you have a question about something or are asked to vote one way or another.

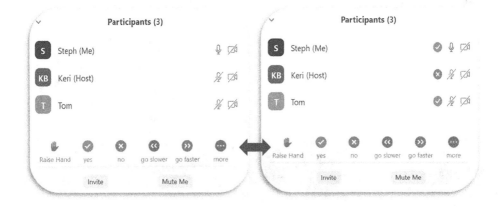

Chat

The chat option allows you to communicate with your fellow attendees in writing. Along with screen sharing, we'll cover this in more depth next.

Record

Attendees have the option to record the meeting on their own computers, as long as the host has enabled that feature. This gives you the chance to go back over everything that was said or shared. Only hosts can record the meeting in the Zoom cloud, so this recording will be saved to your computer, phone, or another device.

Leave Meeting

People attending a meeting can't end it. However, you can leave the meeting at any time, simply by clicking the button.

Functionality

There are some additional functions available to conference call attendees on Zoom. They include the ability to share your screen, as well as message the other people in attendance.

Screen Sharing

Attendees can share their screens with the other people in the meeting.

In order to share your screen on Zoom, you need to be using either the web browser extension or a mobile device app.

Step 1: Click on the meeting control button labeled "Share Screen"

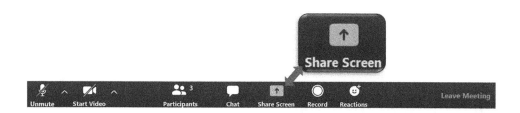

Step 2: Choose which screen that you wish to share. Zoom will give you several different options. Simply click on the one that you want everyone else in the meeting to see. Additional options include showing other apps that you have open on either your phone, computer, or another device that is being used to view the meeting.

Additional Screen Sharing Options

You also have the ability to share sounds from your computer or view full-screen clips, such as videos, through Zoom.

Computer Sound: This option shares all the sounds played by your computer while you're sharing your screen in Zoom. [keyboard sounds, alerts, etc.]

Optimize: When you're playing video clips during your meeting, this option allows you to show them at full-screen size, making them less blurry.

Screen Sharing Tips

Sharing a screen can slow down Zoom. There may be a lag between what is displayed on your screen and when your attendees see it, so keep that in mind when you are presenting.

Don't scroll too fast, as it can be dizzying to your audience.

If you are sharing a word document or a small image, consider using the magnify feature on your computer so that you can 'zoom in' on the content you are showing your audience.

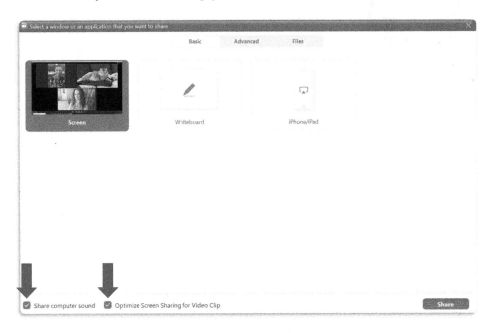

Chat Room and Private Messages

As with screen sharing, you can access the main chat room and share private messages with other participants and the host when you're accessing the Zoom meeting through a mobile device app or your computer browser.

Step 1: Click the "participants" button and then the "chat" button at the bottom of the screen.

Step 2: If you're not in full-screen mode, the chat window will pop up on the right-hand side of the screen. Otherwise, in full-screen mode, the chat window can be moved around on your screen, allowing you to place it where you'd like.

View: not in full screen mode

View: full screen mode

In order to send a message through chat, just type it into the open chat window and press the "enter" key. This sends the message.

If you want to send a private message, click the menu option next to the "To" in the chat window and select the person that the message is intended for. If you don't do this, your message will be seen by everyone in the meeting who has the chat window open.

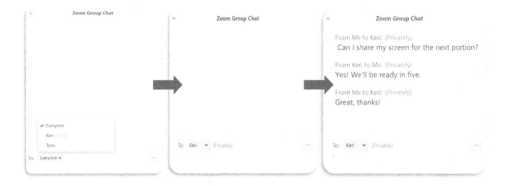

Recipients of chat messages will see a small notification near the bottoms of their screen. However, if that person has the chat window open, it will appear there, instead of as a notification.

Keep in mind that the host of every Zoom meeting or webinar has the ability to turn off chatting and related notifications.

4

Best Practices for Zoom Meetings

Whether you're hosting a Zoom meeting or attending one, there are some general rules that you should adhere to. After all, a business meeting is essentially still a business meeting, even if you're in the comfort of your own home.

From proper Zoom etiquette to dressing properly, there are several things that you need to know before you begin your next conference call, meeting or interview.

Proper Zoom Etiquette

Proper Zoom etiquette involves behaving professionally during your meeting. You don't want to act in a negative manner, as that can be distracting to your colleagues or fellow attendees who are paying attention to the host. Also, if you're the host, you want to leave a good impression on all your attendees.

Test Your Audio and Visual Components

Before joining a Zoom meeting, whether you're hosting or attending, it's important to make sure that your audio and visual components are working properly. There's nothing like getting on the call, only to find that you have technical difficulties and can't communicate with your attendees or view and listen to the host.

If you go to https://www.zoom.us/test, you can join a test meeting. While there, you can see just how well your computer or smartphone's camera, microphone, or speakers work. It's recommended that you do this prior to joining an official meeting.

In addition, it's unprofessional to enter a Zoom room without knowing if you can properly see and hear the host. You wouldn't enter an in-person meeting in this type of disruptive manner, so you certainly shouldn't do it in a virtual conference room. Before telling the host that the sound or video isn't working, double-check your own equipment and settings.

Choose the right location

When you attend a meeting or interview, remember that the video conferencing component of Zoom calls means that people will be able to see behind you into your home, or the office or café you are sitting in.

The best location is one that is as quiet as possible so that when you aren't muted, you aren't also broadcasting sounds from your location. While we all have families and pets, no one wants to hear them in a business meeting or interview. If you are trying to speak over them, your message may be muddy, and you won't be seen and heard as a professional.

Another considering in our selection of your location is your background. What will the other participants see behind you? I am sure you don't want to be sharing your laundry pile behind you and don't want fellow attendees to see all your kid's toys as you attend a meeting. The best location is one with a simple or blank background on the wall behind you. You may find yourself moving around your home to find an appropriate backdrop for the call.

Pay Attention to the Camera When Speaking

It's a common mistake to look at the microphone on your computer, another device or notes on your desk when speaking. Human nature instinctually has you focus on the instrument that you're speaking into. However, this is bad etiquette on Zoom, and it makes it tricky for others to focus on your face. (Not to mention your face may end up out of the shot entirely when you do this.)

Instead, pay attention when you're speaking, whether you're asking a question during the meeting or hosting, and take pains to focus on the camera instead. Looking directly at it will provide those in attendance with the best view of your face, and it will make it seem as though you're paying attention (because you are.)

Leave Your Microphone on Mute

In addition to paying attention to the background, you also need to be cognizant of everyone else on the call. The last you want is to have your kids or your pets interrupt the meeting with questions, pleas for your attention, or barking.

Keyboard sounds and shuffling or crumpling paper can get picked up by your microphone. Eating during a meeting can also be heard. Any of these are unnecessary disruptions to a meeting or presentation. This is why Zoom provides all attendees with the option of leaving their microphones muted during the call. You'll still be able to hear the host or hosts, although no one else will be able to hear you. If you need to ask a question, get the host's attention and permission to interrupt (unless they've asked "if anyone has a question") and then press your space bar key to temporarily unmute your microphone.

Don't Ask "Can You Hear Me?

It seems as though the first thing people do upon joining any type of video or audio-conferencing call is to ask, "can you hear me?" This is just human nature, although it's also very unprofessional, especially if you're joining a meeting in progress and are interrupting the speaker.

Instead, trust that your audio and video capabilities are working properly. Use the Zoom test meeting before your call starts to ensure that you can hear, be heard, and see what's going on in your actual meeting.

Plus, if you go to ask a question and the host can't hear you, they'll let you know. At that point, you can use the Zoom tools to adjust your microphone or simply utilize the chat or private messaging function to ask your question.

Be Cognizant of Your On-Camera Actions

Even though you're focusing on the host, the other people in the meeting can see you. You aren't invisible. Zoom calls are not the time to itch your nose, pluck at your skin, blow your nose, roll your eyes at the host, laugh obnoxiously (unless the host tells a joke) or do anything else that falls into the realm of "unprofessional." If you need to do one of these things, move away from your computer so that you're off-camera, or turn the camera function off, leaving just the audio in place.

Don't Interrupt the Host

As previously stated under "don't ask if anyone can hear you," you don't want to interrupt the host. If you have a question, give the host a signal, such as changing the icon next to your name or using the private messaging or chat options.

Even if you object to what the host is saying, a Zoom meeting is not the best time to state your opinions. Be polite and listen to everything that they have to say, and take notes, if necessary, so that you can state your thoughts on the material later.

Make Good Use of the Chat Function

Zoom's chat function is there for a reason, so make sure to use it. Unless the host disallows the option, you can chat with the other people on the call or send private messages to other attendees. You can even emphasize your agreement with what the host is saying or use the chat function to ask questions about what is being said.

Make sure to use this tool to communicate properly and get the most out of every Zoom meeting.

Use Good Lighting

It's crucial that your lighting is correct so that the other people in the Zoom room can see your face. You also need to know the difference between warm lighting (which has a yellowish tint) and cool lighting (which is bluish.) Warm lighting is welcoming and makes your face light up, while cool lighting can be harsh and draw out shadows. If you plan on hosting a Zoom meeting, you'll probably want to change out your lights or lightbulbs and adjust your lighting so that your attendees can see you clearly. The right lighting (warm) also entices them to pay more attention to your words.

Those attending a Zoom meeting need to have the lights pointing near, not on, their face. This indirect lighting is less harsh and keeps the focus on your face, even though it's not directly on it. Also, the lights should be in front of you, forward-facing, not coming from behind. Any backlighting can create unusual shadows. Also, if you choose to use a ceiling light and sit directly in front of it, your camera will pick up plenty of glare, making you hard to see.

Dress the Part

Your behavior during a Zoom call isn't the only thing that matters. You also need to focus on your attire, your hair, and your makeup. Professional meetings require you to dress the part as well.

While working from home lends itself to wearing gym or sweat clothes, consider the type of meeting or online event you are attending, and dress accordingly. If it's work-related, consider using your organization's casual Friday guidelines.

You don't have to wear simple black and white for your Zoom meeting unless that's what you wear every day to work. Instead, opt for simple, bright colored tops and shirts with patterns that don't turn into optical illusions on camera. You don't want to do draw all the attention to yourself and your clothing, even if you're hosting. You want your attendees to focus on your words. If you're just attending the meeting, you don't want to distract anyone and keep them from paying attention to the host.

Part II
Host Guidelines

5

Setting Up Your Account

Now that you know how to attend a Zoom meeting, it's time to discuss everything that goes into hosting one. You first need to create a Zoom account, which involves going through the prompts, starting with entering your birthday and email address. Follow all the instructions on the screen to get your main account created. Once it's set up, the next step has you set up some general options.

General Options

After signing into your Zoom account, you're greeted with four different options on the home page. They include:

New Meeting: You have the option of starting a new meeting right in Zoom. This means that you are jumping into a meeting right then and there, as long as you know who you wish to speak to.

Join: If you already have a meeting to attend, you can click on the join button. Follow the screen prompts to join any meeting that you've been invited to.

Schedule: Need to schedule a meeting? This button not only lets you pick and date and time, but you can also invite people from there, or grab the meeting ID and send it to the people who you'd like to attend.

Share Screen: You need to have a Zoom meeting ID in order to share your screen in a meeting that has just begun or is in progress. This button goes through the prompts, making it easy to do just that.

Also, on the right-hand side of the screen, you'll see a calendar option that displays the date and time of any meetings that you've already set up or have been invited to. This is a good way to keep an eye on your upcoming meetings and general schedule.

Hosting Meetings Versus Webinars

Zoom has two different platforms that you can choose from - meetings and webinars. Both do very specific things, so it's important to know which one you want when you're setting up your next Zoom event.

When you set up your Zoom account, you'll be asked which type of event you plan on holding. To help you make the correct choice, here are the main differences between the two.

Meetings:

- More interactivity between the attendees

- Good for meetings with customers, holding company training sessions, or any other type of business meeting

- You have several options for your Zoom meeting account, including cost-free plans

- Participants and attendees have more functionality in meetings. They can chat amongst themselves, mute their audio, and more

- Attendees can share their screens in the meeting

Webinars:

- The only people interacting are the hosts and any panelists

- Best for meetings of 50 or more people with that intent of sharing information with the attendees or teaching them something

- You need to pay for the webinar option, and it can either be standalone or as an add-on to your existing account

- Hosts hold all the power in the webinar platform, having the ability to control their own audio and even mute the attendees, who are primarily there to listen

- Only the hosts and panelists can share their screens

Branding and Backgrounds

One of the most interesting things about Zoom is that it provides you with the ability to change your background, allowing you to choose one of the Zoom backgrounds or even upload one that includes your company's branding. You aren't limited to physical things in the room.

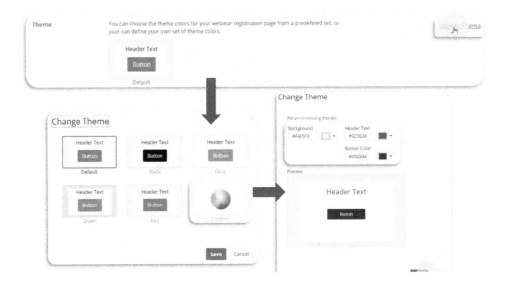

This is as easy as:

Step 1: Log into Zoom

Step 2: Click on Zoom Rooms and then select Room Management

Step 3: Click on Account Management

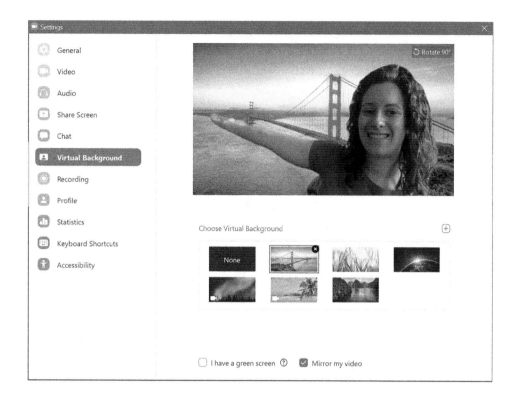

Step 4: Select the "Background Image for Zoom Rooms" option in your Account Profile

Step 5: Select your chosen background and click "open"

Your background image automatically becomes the default for that Zoom room

6

Recording Meetings and Webinars

One of the best things about Zoom is that the platform gives account holders the ability to record their meetings and webinars, saving them to the platform. In order to do so, you first need a Zoom account that includes a storage upgrade. Otherwise, you won't be able to save your Zoom meetings to the cloud.

In addition, if you allow it, your meeting attendees can record the meetings as well. If they don't have an account where they have paid for the cloud storage upgrade, they'll need to save it to their computer or electronic device.

Recording Meetings and Webinars

Recording your meetings and webinars in Zoom is as easy as adjusting your settings and then, when your meeting gets started, setting the recording in motion.

Correcting Your Settings

Step 1: Sign in to Zoom (make sure that you're the admin and can change the account settings)

Step 2: Go to Account Management, from there, go to Account Settings

Step 3: Go to the tab labeled Recording

Step 4: On that tab, check to ensure that the setting for Cloud Recording is turned on

Step 5: If that setting is off, press the toggle until it turns on

Recording a Meeting

Step 1: Host a meeting in Zoom

Step 2: Go to the Zoom meeting toolbar and select the Record button

Step 3: Set it to record to the cloud

Once your recording is in progress, you have the power to either stop or pause it during the meeting. However, clicking on End Meeting will also stop the recording.

Note: Zoom needs to process the recording before you can view it. The recording won't be available immediately after your meeting ends. Instead, you'll have to wait until you get an email from Zoom letting you know that the recording is available.

Storing Recordings

Unless you've chosen local storage (i.e. your computer) as the place to store your recording, Zoom will save your recorded webinar or meeting to the cloud. You can access these recordings by:

Step 1: Logging into Zoom

Step 2: Go to your profile

Step 3: Click "Settings:

Step 4: Select "Recordings"

Step 5: Open the folders

Transcriptions

One of the most interesting things about Zoom is that the platform can transcribe your recordings for you and save them to the cloud along with the recording itself. You can even add the transcription to the recording as a kind of closed captioning.

Start by:

Step 1: Sign in to Zoom (make sure that you're the admin and can change the account settings)

Step 2: Go to Account Management, from there, go to Account Settings

Step 3: Go to the tab labeled Recording

Step 4: On that tab, check to ensure that the setting for Cloud Recording is turned on

Step 5: If that setting is off, press the toggle until it turns on

Step 6: Go to the Advanced settings

Step 7: Select the option for Audio Transcripts

Step 8: Press Save

7

Running a Meeting

Zoom makes running a meeting easy to do. You have everything that you need in order to do so in your account features. However, keep in mind that if you want to run a meeting that's longer than 40 minutes or has a large number of attendees, you'll need one of their paid accounts.

Smaller Zoom meetings (with less than 100 participants) with limited account features, can be run under a free account. However, your functionality is very limited.

Setting Up a Meeting

To set up a meeting, you'll need to have a Zoom account, whether free or paid. It's as easy as:

Step 1: Log into Zoom

Step: Click on "New Meeting"

Your instant meeting will be in progress, and you can add people to it from there.

Scheduling and Invitations

However, if you want to hold a more formal, scheduled meeting, you'll need to follow the prompts on the main account screen to not only schedule it but also invite participants.

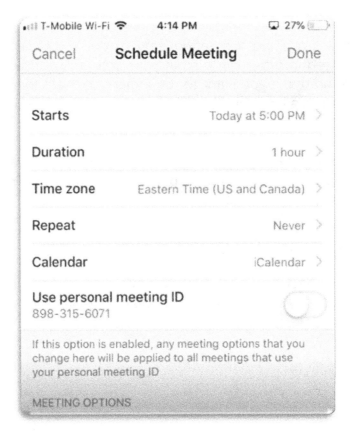

Step 1: Log into Zoom

Step 2: Click on the Schedule icon

Step 3: Enter your information, including your topic, chosen date and time, and your time zone.

Step 4: Set up all of the additional features, including whether or not it will be a video meeting or just an audio one, and whether or not you want the participant's video to be on or off when they join the meeting.

Step 5: Choose your audio options (audio, visual, or both)

Step 6: Click on "Schedule"

Next, you need to invite some participants to your meeting.

Step 1: Log into Zoom or go back your main account screen

Step 2: Click on Meetings

Step 3: Choose your meeting and click on the main topic

Step 4: Copy and paste the meeting invitation

Step 5: Send out the invitation via email to your desired participants

Running Zoom Meetings

On the day of your meeting, spend some time preparing for it. Start by ensuring that you have all the proper settings in place, including your background, branding, and whether or not you want the attendees to pop up on video the minute that they join the meeting.

Also, take the time to test your computer's audio and video functionality so that you don't have to adjust any setting as the meeting begins. This way, you can jump right into it, ready to do.

Finally, be prepared. Your audience doesn't want to see you fumble for things to say. Have a set agenda, some PowerPoint slides, and a general of what you'd like to say to your participants.

Host Controls

There are a number of host controls within a Zoom meeting. Some of them are very similar to the ones used by participants, including the audio and video controls.

Audio Controls

The "mute" and "unmute" button allows you to control whether or not the other people on the call can hear you.

Clicking on the up arrow or caret ^ next to the mute/unmute button gives you control over the speaker and microphone. With it, you can change the audio settings, switch from the built-in speaker to a plug-in one, or turn off the computer audio altogether.

Shortcuts: Instead of clicking the buttons on the screen, you can use the following keyboard shortcuts to mute the audio on your end, leaving the other attendees unable to hear you.

Windows: Alt + A
Mac: Shift + Command + A

If you want to speak, but have the microphone muted, you can press the spacebar key on either type of computer. This will "unmute" your microphone as long as the key is held down. Once you release it, your microphone will be muted again.

Video Controls

Using the video controls, you can control the camera on your computer, preventing other attendees from seeing you. Note that this doesn't affect the audio, so you'll still be able to hear the host and other attendees.

Clicking the "start video" and "stop video" button turns your computer's camera either on or off.

Clicking on the up arrow or caret ^ next to the start/stop video button gives you control over the camera that Zoom has access to. With it, you can change the background to a virtual one included by the program (if the host allows you to do so), switch from one camera to another that's also attached to your computer or device, or turn off the video altogether.

Manage Participants

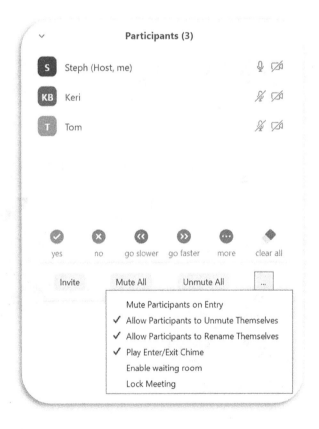

With this option, you can control who is in attendance at the meeting, removing any people who seem to cause problems or shouldn't be present. You also have the ability to invite people to join your meeting or to allow your participants to do the same.

Polling

Hosts have the ability to create polls during a meeting. You can edit and launch the poll as well. This is a good way to see what your audience thinks about a specific topic.

Share Screen

Like the attendees, you can share your screen with everyone watching in order to make a specific point or even have them follow along with an accompanying PowerPoint presentation.

You can share your screen with your attendees in the middle of a meeting by following these steps:

Make sure that you're using either the web browser extension or a mobile device app.

Step 1: Click on the meeting control button labeled "Share Screen"

Step 2: Choose which screen that you wish to share. Zoom will give you several different options. Simply click on the one that you want everyone else in the meeting to see. Additional options include showing other apps that you have open on either your phone, computer, or another device that is being used to view the meeting.

Chat

Hosts have the ability to text chat with the attendees or turn off the option so that the chat room won't open.

Record

This option allows you to control the cloud or local recording of your meeting. You can begin recording, stop the recording, or even pause it midway through.

Closed Captioning

Hosts can allow Zoom to provide closed captioning to attendees for those who may be unable to listen to the meeting.

Breakout Rooms

Hosts can open up breakout rooms during the meeting. We'll go into those in more depth in the next section.

Live

You have two choices to go "live" with your meeting. You can choose to do so on Workplace by Facebook or via a custom streaming service, like YouTube.

End Meeting

Only hosts have the power to end a meeting. Attendees can always leave a meeting at any time.

Break Out Rooms

Break out rooms are used to break the meeting up into smaller groups. To do this, the option first needs to be enabled in your account settings.

Step 1: Log into Zoom as an administrator

Step 2: Go to Account Management and then to Account Settings

Step 3: Click on the Meeting tab and then go to Breakout Room

Step 4: Toggle the setting to on

From that page, you can adjust the breakout room settings to:

- Automatically break the group up evenly and assign them to rooms
- Close the rooms after a certain period of time
- Put the members of a designated group into a room
- Assign registered participants to certain breakout rooms

Messaging

Hosts have the ability to let their participants chat amongst themselves and send private messages. If the messaging option is enabled, you can access it in the following way:

Step 1: Click the "participants" button and then the "chat" button at the bottom of the screen.

Step 2: If you're not in full-screen mode, the chat window will pop up on the right-hand side of the screen. Otherwise, in full-screen mode, the chat window can be moved around on your screen, allowing you to place it where you'd like.

View: not in full screen mode

View: full screen mode

In order to send a message through chat, just type it into the open chat window and press the "enter" key. This sends the message.

If you want to send a private message, click the menu option next to the "To" in the chat window and select the person that the message is intended for. If you don't do this, your message will be seen by everyone in the meeting who has the chat window open.

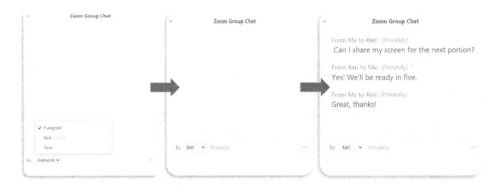

Recipients of chat messages will see a small notification near the bottoms of their screen. However, if that person has the chat window open, it will appear there, instead of as a notification.

8

Hosting a Webinar

Webinars are a great way for a company to build its audience. These more formal meetings limit audience participation, which is great for those who expect more than 100 attendees. A webinar usually consists of the host and a handful of panelists (optional) who present the information to the participants. With a webinar, the participants are not on the screen, only the host and the presentation.

Setting Up a Webinar

Setting up a webinar is fairly simple. First, make sure that your account is enabled for them. You'll need either the webinar add-on feature or a just a webinar Zoom account

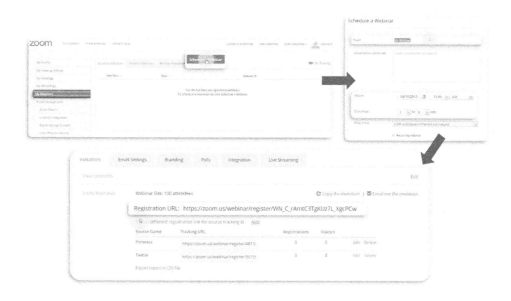

Step 1: Log into Zoom

Step 2: Choose the Webinars option

Step 3: Schedule your webinar

Step 4: Invite people to it or place a link on your website allowing people to register for your webinar

How do you do that? Here are the instructions:

Step 1: Log into Zoom or go back your main account screen

Step 2: Click on Webinars

Step 3: Choose your meeting and click on the main topic

Step 4: Copy and paste the webinar invitation

Step 5: Send out the invitation via email to your desired participants

Using Access Codes

You have the option of requiring participants to preregister for your webinar by either using an email invitation or a special access code. This way, you can approve (or not approve) who attends, sell access to the webinar to raise money for your company, and ensure that those who shouldn't have access, can't see your webinar.

Start by:

Step 1: Sign in to Zoom as someone with Account Management capabilities

Step 2: Click on Account Settings

Step 3: Go to the Meeting tab

Step 4: In the dropdown, make sure that the password setting is toggled on

Step 5: Lock the setting

Now, it's time to set up the access code or password:

Step 1: Sign in to Zoom

Step 2: Go to your Webinars

Step 3: Click on the Webinar that you'll be restricting access to

Step 4: Click on Edit

Step 5: Change the password

Step 6: Hit the Save button

Live Streaming

Webinars are often live-streamed. This means that the participants are watching in real-time. In addition to having an audience through the Zoom platform, you can enable your webinar to be live streamed on YouTube and Facebook. This gives you a much larger audience.

Note: You'll need a YouTube account in order to enable this option.

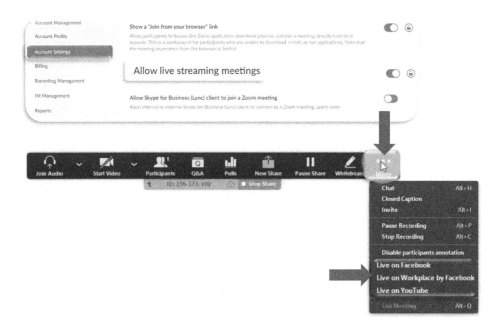

Step 1: Sign in to Zoom and make sure that you're an administrator on the account

Step 2: Go to Account Management and then Account Settings

Step 3: Go to the Advanced Tab and enable YouTube

Step 4: Before your webinar is underway, go live on YouTube by clicking on the Custom Live Streaming option and entering your YouTube key

9

Tips from Top Experts

We asked a few experts for their advice on how to look your best on zoom, whether you are attending a meeting, leading a meeting, making a presentation or being interviewed by the media, you'll want to look like a Hollywood star or a true professional on Zoom.

• ●————————● •

Alyssa Peek, A virtual presence coach, headshot photographer, and artist offers these top **tips for a powerful presence to lead with impact**:

Set Up

- Decide what room is best for your workspace. The room should be private (if possible).
- Make sure your face is well lit. The light source, window or lamp, should be facing you, not behind you.
- Place the camera at eye level. Use books or props to raise it.
- Have a clean and organized background. Remove any distractions.
- Good posture is key to looking confident on camera. Use a pillow for lumbar support to keep you upright or stand.
- Dress appropriately from waist up for your meeting or interview.

Zoom Etiquette

- Have a profile picture associated with your account.
- When excusing yourself during a group meeting, select "stop video" and your profile photo will appear, so your presence is still felt. Select "start video" once you return to the meeting.
- Don't walk around with your laptop with video on. Do as above.

NOTE: you must also mute yourself when you stop video otherwise the sound will still be on.

- Mute yourself unless speaking so outside noise doesn't disturb others i.e., keyboard clacking, sirens, kids, dogs.
- Refrain from eating on camera. Drinks are acceptable. If you must eat, do as above.

Bonus Tips:

1. Under the Video Settings tab, select "Touch up my appearance" for skin smoothing.

2. When using Zoom on your phone, your image will not appear on the /your screen, but your camera is still ON. *Be aware!

Monisha Kapur, A virtual personal stylist, style coach, speaker, author and founder of 344pm.com offers these **tips on style**:

Wardrobe and Style

Working from home alone can lead to a loss of efficiency, so to help stay productive avoid wearing loungewear and instead opt for comfortable workwear.

Studies have shown that what you wear to work, even when you work from home, has an effect on your productivity, mood, preparedness and confidence. While the setting is different, the work you do is the same, and it's important to project a sense of professionalism, especially if you lead a team.

Here are some things consider when choosing your work from home outfit:

- Dress to your personal style and brand to portray poise and leadership externally and confidence internally.
- Be Comfortable- Comfort is key. Wear clothing that incorporates a stretch fabric, like spandex, it's not only comfortable but helps creates a polished look.
- Layer- Keep a few professional clothing items, like blazers, ties and accessories handy in your home office area. This way you can be Zoom call ready at a moment's notice.
- Dress for the day- Check your schedule for the day and dress accordingly.

Dress for a Zoom meeting – from home or a cafe

- A work meeting- It's important to project your authentic personal brand, even on a Zoom call. When working from home or a café you don't have to dress in a suit and tie (unless you want to) but wearing professional yet comfortable clothing is the way to go. Think, elevated basics (i.e.- black pants, comfortable button downs, silk tees), fabrics with stretch and clothes that fit you well.

- For women- Pair a work blouse in a fun print with Ponte fabric pants and a duster for layering. Or a chambray button down shirt, a neck scarf and a knit midi skirt. A solid color jumpsuit layered with an animal print button down shirt is another option.

- For Men- Pair a button-down shirt in a multi-color check print, khaki pants and an unstructured blazer or V-neck sweater for

65

layering. Or a clean polo shirt in a pop color with dark denim. Staying with the dark denim, you could wear that with a well-fitting cotton / spandex blend tee with and a button-down shirt for layering.

Makeup and Accessories

- If you normally wear makeup and accessories when you work outside your office, then definitely continue when you work from home. This will help keep you in "work mode"
- To be more comfortable you may want to choose lighter make up and easy to layer accessories like scarves or necklaces.
- Be mindful of where your mic is and avoid necklaces that hit up against the mic, or scarves covering the mic.
- Avoid clanky accessories like bracelets and earrings.

Color and print patterns

- For everyday Zoom meetings it's OK to wear a bright color or a non-distracting print. Wearing bright colors can help boost your mood so they're perfect for working from home.
- For video interviews, or job interviews stick with solid colors.

Pro Tip: Be aware of which colors work best for your skin tone to avoid looking washed out on camera.

Kathryn Janicek, A media and public speaking trainer who teaches executives who need to do interviews on TV stations worldwide through video conferencing offers these **tips on making a good impression through video conferencing:**

Background

The key to speaking on stage, in the media, in your videos, during live video conferencing and in job interviews is to keep the audience focused on your message and nothing else. Create a background that isn't distracting.

Look at the wall or space behind you and make sure nothing behind you is distracting. Look for light switches, outlets, open doors, open windows, and anything else that could be distracting.

You want people to remember your content and message, and if there's a very obvious picture or book behind you that grabs the viewers' focus -- remove it. You don't want anything in the background distract from your message, or worse, offend your audience.

Lighting

When you are selling your company, your brand, a product or service - you want to be seen in the best light. Literally and figuratively.

When you show up in a media interview or a meeting and you are poorly lit or there are lots of shadows on your face, the audience can subconsciously feel like you're hiding something. That you can't be trusted. Good lighting is your best friend.

The majority of your message is your physical content. This is why what you do, and your appearance is just as important, if not more, than what you say.

Lighting is vital to the way you appear on the screen. Make sure there are no windows behind you. The lighting needs to be in front of you. Natural light from a window is the best. If you don't have a room that works for this, use soft lighting from a lamp and place it right in front of you without creating shadows from your monitor or phone. I've used

Position the camera at eye level

Before you jump on a call, make sure the audience will not be looking up your nose or at your ceiling. We've seen a lot of these kinds of calls and interviews!

Make sure you're going to appear to your audience at the angle they're used to seeing you from across a table. Adjust your computer so it's at eye level by adding books or something else to raise the computer up a little.

Sit upright, in the front half of your chair, and look alert. Do not swivel. when you're speaking.

Make eye contact with the camera

Just like in person, you want to make great eye contact with your audience. When you're video conferencing, this can be tough. The software will show you speaking on your monitor, along with the person interviewing you - or all the people you're talking to on the call. This can create a lot of distractions for you.

The key here is to make sure when you are talking, you look into the camera on your computer or phone. When you look directly into the camera, you will be appearing as if you're looking right into the eyes of your audience. This takes practice to get it down and not let your eyes wander off and look at all the other people on the call.

Why is this so important? When you let your eyes move from person to person or somewhere else in your room, you may appear to be insincere, detached, uninterested, insecure and even shifty. Make time to practice good eye contact. You do not want to portray the message that you don't care about the meeting or interview.

Be camera-ready

Working from home means you may not have to put a lot of focus on what you're wearing on your lower half, but you need to make sure that from waist up, you're all business.

Take the time before an on-camera meeting to do your hair, makeup and wear something that is not too distracting. For on-camera media interviews through video conferencing, my clients normally have their makeup and hair professionally done.

It may not be possible to have someone come to your house to get that done. There are many consultants who can talk you through this virtually right now.

If you don't have a professional to help you, make sure you look well-rested, alert, your skin looks healthy and your best features are emphasized. Since you want your audience to lock-in with your eyes and trust you.

Make sure your eyes are not blocked by extra hair and eyeglass frames that don't fit your face properly.

Both men and women can benefit from a little concealer under their eyes.

Make sure your hair isn't distracting and falling into your face during your calls and try not to adjust your hair or touch your face while you're on camera.

When it comes to wardrobe, it's better to wear a solid color or something that's not as distracting. If you have a bold or quirky personality and you love bright colors and patterns, it's okay to be yourself, just make sure you don't distract from the conversation.

Be heard! (and sometimes silent)

If you're in a virtual meeting with a lot of other people, mute yourself when you're not talking. You may have kids and/or pets at home right now and a spouse working from home.

This is the time to learn how to effectively mute yourself when you're not talking so the speaker is heard clearly. Also, make sure you shut off your notifications on both your computer and phone. You don't want to hear your computer or phone dinging throughout a call or interview. You also could be taking notes during the call, and you don't want the sound of your fingers tapping away to distract the others.

10
Conclusion

Now that you understand many of the basics of Zoom, it's time to take your usage to the next level. This book has covered topics starting with what the platform does to the many different ways to access and participate in a Zoom call. You know what to wear and how to behave during your conference calls, as well as how to host both a Zoom meeting and a webinar.

Hopefully this knowledge of how Zoom works and how to use it, will help you feel comfortable and confident participating in and hosting online events. It should also allow you to focus on the content, and not the technology.

If you have any additional questions about Zoom, please head to the next section, where we've answered some of the frequently asked questions we get. They'll provide you with more knowledge regarding this amazingly useful, cloud-based platform.

For additional training visit our website at PlainJanesGuide.com

Resources

Here are some resources that may enhance your Zoom experience. Most are optional, however if you are hosting a meeting, being interviewed by the media or a prospective employer, you'll want to consider these upgrades to help you look your best online.

Support

If you need additional Zoom support visit their website at: https://support.zoom.us/hc/en-us

Training

For video-based training on Zoom – www.plainjanesguide.com
For custom training and workshops contact http://www.janetabachnick.com

Products /Equipment

For many Zoom users, there is no extra equipment needed as their computers, tablets and phones have the right capabilities. There are upgrades and optional addons you may want to purchase. Amazon and B & H Photo www.bhphotovideo.com have large selections.

I am not going to make specific product recommendations. Both Amazon and B &H offer a wide range of products in all price ranges, along with product reviews so you can evaluate for yourself. Instead here is some guidance as to what to search for.

Cameras

Search for 'webcam' and you will find appropriate cameras for Zoom and online video conferencing.

Audio

There are a variety of types of microphones to select from. There are desktop models, headsets, earbuds and attachments for your phone. Search for 'zoom', 'livestreaming', 'podcasting' microphones. Also search for 'headset with microphone'.

Lighting

There are a lot of lighting options, from lamps you can repurposein your home to those designed just for livestreaming and video recording.

Search for "video conference lighting' and 'lighting for video recording' or 'lighting for selfies' and borrow from home contractors for a very affordable 'clamp lamp light'.

Zoom Backgrounds

There are two types of backgrounds that you can use with online meetings.

Photos can be uploaded to your Zoom account to create a background for your online meeting. For free professional quality photos with full usage rights visit Pexels [http://pexels.com] and Unsplash [http://www.unsplash.com]

Photo backdrops can be positioned behind you to create the illusion of a different space or room. They come as freestanding ones on frames, and others that can be tacked on to the wall behind you. They come in patterns such as brick walls and reclaimed wood to full rooms, offices and locations. Search for 'photo backdrop', 'photo background', 'vinyl backdrop for photo studio' and 'video background.'

Custom backgrounds can be with photos or graphically designed. Create one using Canva.com or you can hire a designer to create one for you.

Services

Professional Virtual Style Assistance – Monisha Kapur, 344 PM

Monisha Kapur, is a virtual personal stylist, style coach, speaker, author and founder of 344pm.com works with women entrepreneurs and executives to help them find their signature style so they can confidently showcase their personal brand. She provides women with one-on-one virtual wardrobe consultations that are tailored to their individual budget, personal style, and body. For more information visit: http://www.344pm.com/

Zoom Virtual Presence Session – Alyssa Peek, Peek Photography

Alyssa Peek is a virtual presence coach, headshot photographer and artist. She offers one-on-one virtual sessions on how to elevate your virtual presence and "set the stage" for your virtual video calls at home, with "camera ready" style to stand out and be seen online.

To book a personalized Virtual Presence Coaching Session visit: https://calendly.com/alyssapeek/virtual-presence-session

On-Camera Professional Media Training – Kathryn Janicek, Producing the Best YOU

Kathryn Janicek is an Emmy Award-Winning media trategist, public speaking trainer and video producer. She trained on-air talent, producers, and writers before switching her focus to helping entrepreneurs, corporate executives, healthcare experts, major companies and professional athletes.

For more information visit: http://www.kathrynjanicek.com/

Branded Zoom Backdrops – Lara Kisielewska, Optimum Design & Consulting

Optimum Design & Consulting can create a customized background for your Zoom calls so that you stand out from others. Express your brand personality using your logo and other branding elements — be it clever and fun, polished and professional, or friendly and engaging. Backdrops can incorporate contact info to make it easy for others to connect when networking online. For more information e-mail: lara@optimumdc.com

Transcribing Recordings

If you want to transcribe your recording after you have downloaded it from Zoom, here are a few good resources.

Rev [http://www.rev.com] Affordable and fast transcription by humans starting at $1.25 per minute.

Otter [http://www.otter.ai] off ers rapid machine transcription with 600 free minutes. They also off er Live Video Meeting Notes for Zoom in their premium plans.

Bonus Add-on

We recognize that each of us learn in different ways, with different learning styles. To provide you with additional support, we will be offering additional, video-based training online.

As a thank you for purchasing this book, we'd like to show you our appreciation. Join us for our video-based training on Zoom Meetings. Get a 50% discount on our online training.

Visit: PlainJanesGuide.com
Coupon Code: ZOOMBOOK

FAQs

There are many different questions that people have about using Zoom. In this section, we're going to go through many frequently asked questions and answer them to clear things up for you. Hopefully, some of the many questions that you have after going through this book will be answered here.

Do You Need a Zoom Account to Attend a Meeting?

No, if you're just going to attend a meeting as a general participant, then you don't need a Zoom account. Also, attending meetings either through your place of employment or as a free webinar doesn't cost anything. The only time you'll need to pay to attend something is if it's a webinar done through Zoom that charges for attendance. And even then, that fee goes to the company hosting the webinar, not Zoom itself.

How Do I Attend a Meeting?

You should have gotten an invitation to your meeting or webinar, which includes a link to the event and other access details. Sometime a host may only send the link. It may also include an access code, which you will need to input once Zoom asks for it.

Do I Need Any Software to Use Zoom?

As we mentioned, you don't need an account to attend a Zoom meeting, webinar or interview, however you will need to download the software. Once you click on the meeting link you were provided by your host, it will prompt the software to download, and it will then open the meeting.

What if I Don't Have a Camera in my Computer or Phone?

You can use an external camera that plugs into your computer or phone. We have some general equipment recommendations in the Resource section.

Do I Have to Be on Camera?

Technically the answer is no, you don't have to be on camera; Zoom gives the user control over whether they want to use the video feature and be on camera. If you are required to attend a work meeting, an interview or other business event, you will most likely be expected to be on camera along with the other participants.

How Do I Get into or Out of Full Screen Mode?

To go into full screen mode, simply bring your mouse to the top right corner of the Zoom room and click on the icon that looks like 4 arrows.

To exit full screen mode, you can mouse over the same location and click 'exit full screen or use the Esc button on your keyboard.

Can I Change My Background as an Attendee?

To change your Zoom background, you need to have a Zoom account. This means that people attending a conference call or webinar simply by entering the specific meeting ID number don't have the ability to change their backgrounds. Also, backgrounds are set only by the host, who has the ability to set what their attendees see behind them. You also need to have a device that meets the standards Zoom requires to enable backgrounds.

I Don't Want People to See into My House – How do I Use Zoom?

There are a few options that you can use to ensure that people don't see into your home or location. The first one is to position yourself so you are close to a blank wall. You can check what will be visible to other Zoom participants by enabling your webcam and checking the view prior to the meeting and adjust as needed. The other options are to a photo background if settings allow, or a photo backdrop.

Can Anyone Host a Webinar?

No, you need to have a paid Zoom account with the special webinar license to host a webinar. There are several different levels of this paid feature available, depending on the number of people that you plan to have in attendance.

Why Does My Screen Look Different Than What You Show in This Guide?

There are several possible reasons including:

- Zoom has had an update and changed the layout or features
- You are subscribed to a different service level
- You are viewing Zoom on a different device than what we show [our screenshots are all taken from the desktop/laptop view.
- You have chosen a different 'view' once in a Zoom meeting room

Why Can't I See the Controls?

There are times when the Zoom controls seem to disappear. Simply mouse over the bottom of your Zoom room and the features bar should become visible. If you are in full screen mode, you can exit out of it to see all the controls.

Why is My Picture Narrow Compared to Other Attendees?

The most common answer to this is that you are attending a Zoom meeting via your phone.

About Plain Jane's Guides

Plain Jane's Guides is a new imprint of Simply Good Press. It was created to provide easy to follow books on software and technology for non-techie entrepreneurs and small business owners. ZOOM MEETINGS is the first book from this new imprint.

To further assist our readers in their journey, Plain Jane's Guides will also offer online video-based training as a companion to our published books.

To find out about our other books and our online training visit http://plainjanesguides.com

About the Author

Author Jane Tabachnick has introduced thousands of people to new technologies. She has produced conferences and designed online training to introduce entrepreneurs and small businesses to technology and online marketing. She was named one of the Top 100 People Online by Fast Company, and her colleagues call her the 'tech tool guru'.

A content strategist, digital publicity mentor and book publisher, she is the founder of Jane Tabachnick & Co. and Simply Good Press Publishing. She helps entrepreneurs and brands become thought leaders, sharing their message more widely via content, becoming authors and leveraging public relations.

Jane has been featured in Inc, Business Insider, Women's Wear Daily, Addicted2Success, Thrive Global, Business2Community, Crain's New York, Environmental Leader and other media.

She has spoken at Social Media Week – NYC, Indie Author Day, DesignXChange, The Self-Publishing Conference and had been interviewed on a number of podcasts. You can listen to Jane on her micro-podcast **The PR Authority Minute** www.PRAuthorityMinute.com

An adjunct professor at the Fashion Institute in NYC, Jane teaches Sustainable Design Entrepreneurship.

Jane is available for speaking, workshops and trainings. Contact her via her website www.janetabachnick.com

CPSIA information can be obtained
at www.ICGtesting.com
Printed in the USA
LVHW101818010920
664770LV00007BA/387